YOU CAN DANCE

— WITH THE STARS —

In An Environment Of Competitiveness

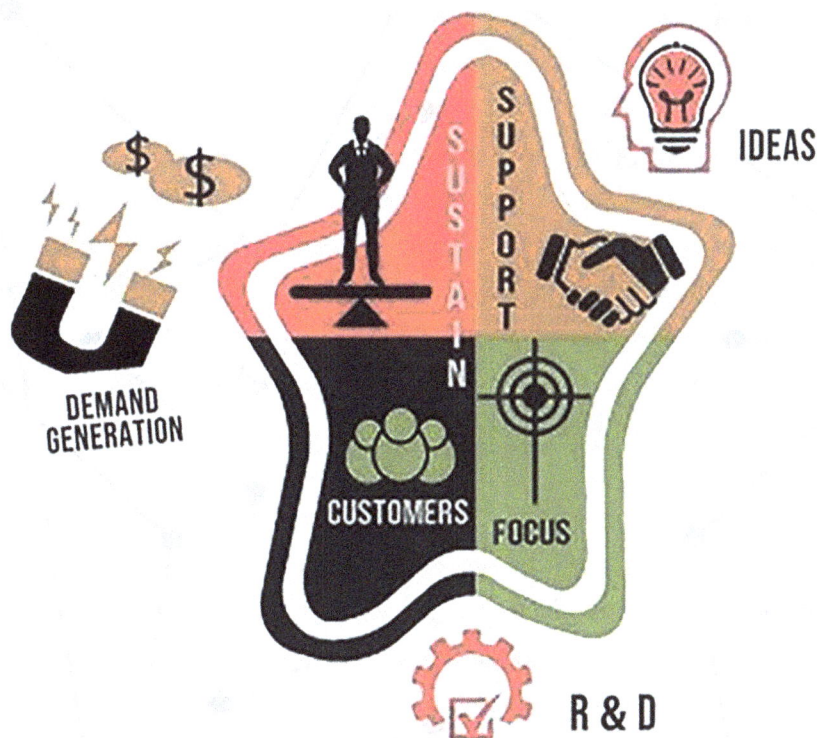

SUSTAIN

SUPPORT

IDEAS

DEMAND GENERATION

CUSTOMERS

FOCUS

R & D

RECOMMENDED

— BY —

Solomon B. Babajide

WORKBOOK PRESS LLC
187 E Warm Springs Rd,
Suite B285, Las Vegas, NV 89119, USA

Website:	https://workbookpress.com/
Hotline:	1-888-818-4856
Email:	admin@workbookpress.com

Ordering Information:
Quantity sales. Special discounts are available on quantity purchases by corporations, associations, and others. For details, contact the publisher at the address above.

Library of Congress Control Number:

ISBN-13:   978-1-961845-18-3 (Paperback Version)
            978-1-961845-19-0 (Digital Version)

PUB.DATE: 06/05/2023

YOU CAN DANCE WITH THE STARS
...In An Environment Of Competitiveness

- GEMS for Business & Ministry Success

CONTENTS

Prologue

This book has been put together to provide quick guidance on those topical issues Christians, including those in ministry and business and those intending to be, have faced down through the ages.

Through my years of being a Christian, businessman, and a pastor, I realize and believe that each of us has a page on God's Master Plan that details the specific purpose of our being, for the common good of his creation. God formed us, determined our purpose, and equipped us to fulfill that plan and purpose. It is wise for each person to search out from the heart of God, his plan and purpose for them. He will oblige.

Topics covered here are brief guidelines to help in making your business and ministry succeed. For a detailed or expanded version of these topics, reach out to IDEAS DEFINITION GLOBAL at IdeasDefinition@gmail.com.

As a result of the above, thoughtful consideration has been given to the use of the words: entrepreneur, enterprise, business, ministry, organization, calling and brand. "You will note that in several instances throughout this book, these words have been interchangeably used, so that the reader could better grasp the significance of the presentation."

Solomon B. Babajide

ABOUT SOLOMON B. BABAJIDE…

Solomon has been on multiple international boards in diverse industries including manufacturing, finance, and service—both for-profit as well as non-profit.

He is acknowledged as specializing in starting organizations, raising them to successful operational levels, and providing direction to management executives that continue to sustain them, most of the time under his supervision.

Solomon served as Group Coordinator for Seaboard Corporation's Nigeria operations (Life Flour Mill Limited, Top Feeds Limited, and Delta Packaging Company Limited) in 1998. Still, he continued to offer his extensive management experience as a business coach to several business initiatives, locally and internationally.

In the corporate world, Solomon's well versed expertise ensures that help is available to his mentees, so they are successful, and their businesses or ministries are sustained into the future.

His academic credentials, coupled with his experience, enable him to train other entrepreneurs in tested, practical methods.

Solomon enjoys developing people and building organizations. He shares his diversified management experience through coaching classes. He helps Christian entrepreneurs battling business failures and sustainability attain relevance, realize long-term success, and grow and scale their businesses and brands into the future.

Solomon Babajide has attended high-level management courses

designed for Chief Executives. He is a Fellow of the Association of Business Executives of the United States of America, an Executive Council Member of the American Institute of Management, a Member, British Institute of Management, a Member of the Nigerian Institute of Management. And a Member of the Chartered Institute of Administration.

He holds a Master's in Business Administration [MBA], a Master's in Economics and Social Development, and an honorary Doctorate in Theology.

Christians need to acknowledge the importance of their faith in everything they do, realizing that they face a competitive world around them. What's more, believers need to be encouraged to understand that business and ministry's success, growth and sustainability give glory to God.

Solomon is the author of the book **YOU CAN MAKE A DETERMINED DIFFERENCE... In An Environment Of Competitiveness.**

In his book, he discusses how everyone should believe in staying focused and determined rather than engaging in "quick fixes" that come from shortcuts. He assists startups and struggling businesses to recognize purpose and relevance.

His other book, **YOU CAN DANCE WITH THE STARS ... In An Environment Of Competitiveness**, inspires entrepreneurs to work and pray because successful business and ministry are never the exclusive preserve of the rich and graduates from ivy-league institutions. Every entrepreneur could aspire and dance with industry stars: in business as well as in ministry.

He knows experientially that businessmen and women, as well as those in ministry, the world over, desire to grow and outlive their enterprises, but few intentionally follow the "how" to realize the desire.

Despite his very busy schedule, Solomon serves the Lord and others in the Christian ministry as Administrator and Pastor of Christ's Ambassadors Ministries in Boston, Massachusetts.

ABOUT IDEAS DEFINITION GLOBAL...

IDEAS Definition Global is a faith-based career and business coaching initiative, founded by Solomon Babajide. Its mission is to encourage people to be who God created them to be and function to their greatest ability in a world full of competition and distractions.

The firm encourages continuous growth, provides motivation, gives support, and solicits unwavering faith.

Solomon shares that hard work and perseverance alone, as important as they are, do not lead to success. Despite making enormous efforts, people do not always receive their desired results. In situations like this, it is easy to lose hope and to quit. IDEAS DEFINITION GLOBAL will stand by you, and like your tour guide on an uncharted path, guide you through the rough terrain until you realize your destiny.

Visit his website: www.IDEASDefinition.com to learn more on how to start, grow, and sustain your enterprise.

"IDEAS Definition Global is set up to coach entrepreneurs in business and ministry that are battling failures and sustainability on how to succeed and to grow and scale their enterprise — into the future, in a world that is full of competition and distractions, so they can break from the status quo.

------- O N E -------

Five Quick and Easy Guides To Having Sustainable, Relevant, Successful Enterprise

Have you ever thought, "If only I could be sure that my business will succeed long-term, like those business giants out there"? If so, this might be the most important report you read all year. Here's why...

HAVE YOU EVER SAID ANY OF THESE THINGS?

- I don't know what to do to keep my business steady and successful far into the future...

- I don't know what to do to find an enduring solution to the threat of competition...

- I'm afraid my business might end up being one of the 96% of businesses that fail...

- I don't know if what I am doing will continue to meet needs long-term...

- I don't have loyal clients/customers/patrons to guarantee my business sustainability...

- I don't know if I have an effective business succession plan in place...

- I am not sure what options are available to me: selling my skill/business/brand or a merger...

- I am afraid that my business might not even be relevant in the years to come.

…If you can relate to any of these, then this guidebook will be life-changing for you.

Realize that owning a business or ministry is hard but running either one is more challenging than you can imagine. Making and sustaining your place in industry is never child's play. This journey of making your mark in whatever enterprise you are in comes with a lot of hard work. And even if you have a breakthrough for your brand, you may still have to compete with the big players in the market, so you owe it to yourself to learn to stay ahead. If you don't work with a planned mindset when working alongside your competition, you might lose your success.

WHAT YOU'RE GOING TO GET...

In this book, you are going to get rare gems and discover the top 5 ways to keep your enterprise relevant, sustained, and dance with the stars fast! It will no longer be a journey of uncertainty and fear; rather, it will be a discovery of your exact business purpose, with full clarity, a blueprint, and passion to pursue your vision at full thrust.

Before I unpack the specifics, I want you to consider for a moment the results of doing nothing. Ignoring a problem doesn't make it go away. It makes the problem worse! How bad could it get? Well, if you ignore the ominous signs of business failures, these are the long-term results you are very likely to get:

• Your efforts in starting the business could fail (worst-case outcome scenario).

- You will continue to feel frustrated and unfulfilled, never being able to tap into your God-given destiny and purpose.

- Your hard-earned investment will be at risk.

- You will deny yourself the opportunity to have the impact, influence, and continued income that you and your business truly deserve.

- Your good intentions could still end up in a catastrophe.

WHY SHOULD YOU LISTEN TO ME?

Some years back, I had the privilege of managing a relatively large packaging company. There were several plants in the country, but we were the second largest—at the time. It was dogged by several market complexities: location, competition, product counterfeiting, growth, etc. A few months after I took it over and with a turn-around strategic plan in place, we increased capacity, reduced cost, expanded market, secured loyal customers, and were on our way to beating the competition. In a short space of time we became the largest single packaging plant of its type—worldwide.

Once the plant was stable, I moved on to help a start-up. The non-profit was struggling and feared it might close. Again, by identifying what the issues were and coming up with my 5-step action plan, the start-up scaled to become one of the largest home healthcare agencies in the community. serving and meeting stakeholders' interests.

I know what to look for in a business and have the ability to propose a clear, confident, and enduring blueprint to scale it forward.

I have been there, and done it. I have developed and managed businesses—large and small, for-profit and not-for-profit—from the ground up. I have experienced the gains of business success and have felt the pains and hurts when they came. I have helped to bring life and relevance to dying enterprises.

It feels good to succeed and stay successful and hurts to not have an assurance of continuity, far into the future. I have hands-on experience, working up through the ranks, and I know with certainty what it takes to keep business doors open and to strengthen weak investments into a sustainable future.

Now let's look at the top 5 ways to make your enterprise sustainable and relevant so your business and/or ministry can dance with the stars.

If you will apply these guidelines, you will in no time begin your journey to relevance, breathe a sigh of relief from the relentless tugging threats into realizing purpose and enduring success. What's more, it will become clear that you are indeed a blessing to humanity, as you are predestined to be.

PAIN POINTS	CURRICULUM	SUCCESS & SUSTAINABILITY
SUSTAINABILITY	It turns out that... simple PROGRAMS do not hold enduring promise to deliver change.	TRANSFORMS into...
MANAGEMENT		
RELEVANCE	ONLY the customizable...	
STABILITY		
STUCK	ideas	**VISION REALIZED**
FINANCING		
TAXES		
WORK-LIFE BALANCE	**CLARITY** on status **MISSION** implementation **VISION** realization **SPIRITUAL** guidance	
RELATIONSHIP		
SUCCESSION	CONFIDENCE COMPETENCE	
PATRONAGE		
TRUST		
ACCOUNTING	**INCREASED SKILL SET**	

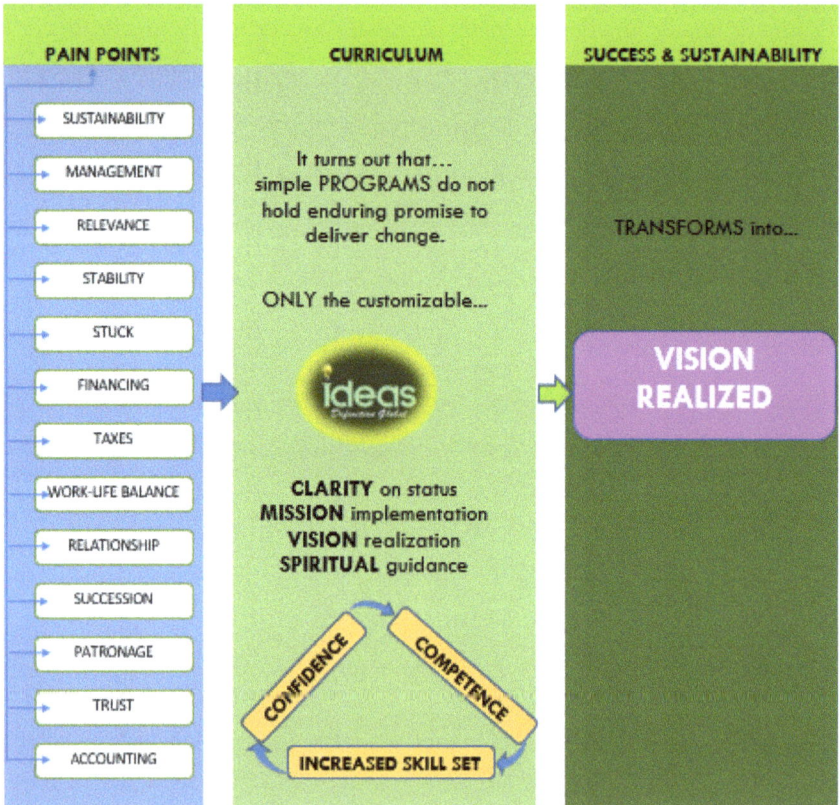

You are not alone in these PAIN points.
But you can CHOOSE to break lose from them
and begin to realize God's plan for you.

1.   Define your Business's Value Proposition. . .

Every enterprise or business is set up to fulfill a purpose, or better yet, to meet specific needs. Entrepreneurs believe they have all the details of what that need is and how it is measured. But many fall far short and have their expectations dashed. And like the saying goes: "you don't know what you don't know."

The expression "put your money where your mouth is" makes little or no sense when the fundamental questions of what the need is and how it should be measured are put to the test and found wanting. I have had business friends whose feasibility studies projected rosy and long-term returns only to be disappointed to find out those were true only on paper but not in market reality. They missed out on the core values, summed up in relevance!

A few years ago, I was invited to invest in a seemingly profitable business. The principal was convinced that his prior few years' returns were indications of much better future returns and so began to market for greater involvement—privately, based on what were short-term gains. Like me, others were invited, and they obliged our business friend. But I did not because from what I gathered, his business was far more of a paper-adherence proposition than a value-based proposition. They tried to work the business plan but failed to take into account those necessary factors of value proposition: filling the need, specifics of added benefit, and the reason their product differs from similar products on the market.

I was proved right a couple of years later, but the damage had been done, which will take a longer time to undo. Obviously, this entrepreneur was more concerned about growing his business by raising money to procure more machinery and expand the building than through the organic path of building an ever-improving product for an ever-expanding market.

2.   Get Better to Get Bigger. . .

Many well-meaning entrepreneurs have sleepless nights desiring but never realizing growth. They want to expand to wider markets and beat the competition. They want to be bigger and so they solicit and pour more money into machinery and equipment, with the aim of widening market share. They focus on brand loyalty, hoping that their customers will stick with them long-term, no matter what. Yet, they fail to take an honest look at what they are offering, what could naturally spur growth, what in their operation works and what doesn't. They neither identify weaknesses nor ask what needs to be improved.

All through my years of business management practice, I believe that enduring success is achieved through a continuous quest for improvement. I have advocated and witnessed bigger always accompanied better. Get better and "the angel" bigger will follow.

3.   Plan for Later. . .By Planning Now!

A good many enterprises are built on immediacy. They follow the dictum to "act now for now." "If it makes money now," they say, "make it." Not much time or thought is given to sustainability. Entrepreneurs that are concerned about making it work only now, irrespective of future consequences, most often find their businesses drag and fail. It is simply like building on quicksand with no solid foundation.

By contrast, business structures that will endure the test of market volatility are built on solid, deep, and well-thought-out and well-laid foundations. Weak and faulty foundations are responsible for 96% of start-ups failing within the first ten years. Such enterprises are anxious to make it work in the short-term, even when a bleak future stares them in the face with almost clear certainty.

The planning-for-later, planning-now concept involves thinking beyond the momentary gains to the needed sacrifices for realizing future gains and stability. And it is the essential building block for growing and scaling businesses. This is the reason God's word encourages to count the cost first before embarking on building a tower (Luke 14:28).

4.   Be Involved, Be Committed, Be Authentic

A few of my business friends prefer to take the path of ease once they have set up their new enterprise. They leave the new baby in the care of "nannies" and "care-takers" and expect to be called periodically to receive dividend checks. And when that does not happen in the manner and size they expect, they consider that they perhaps are in the wrong business and need to make a change. Pivoting in such an instance may not always be the solution. Involvement, commitment, and authenticity always are.

The business suffers when an entrepreneur is not involved, to a good extent, to lead their vision. It also suffers when they show up infrequently and are not committed; but perhaps most devasting is when there is an environment of doubt around the entrepreneur's leadership. Authenticity in business prevents it from floundering and failing. That is where organizational cultures are built and emulated, passed down through the years, and made part of the brand. An entrepreneur with good ideals sows the seed of how it should be done and how others in the system can evangelize on the ideals.

5. Above All, Get Wisdom + Strategy

Wise strategy is never common. Christian entrepreneurs get blind-sided on the importance of wisdom in planning, to their peril. Wise strategy doesn't come easy either.

For several months, one of my businesses suffered continued production decline, despite my management's strict adherence to a machinery maintenance schedule. My team seemed surprised that the machines would act this way, contrary to what the manufacturer suggested in the manual.

It became obvious that this was no longer a typical industry issue. Plus, we did not have a ton of money needed to replace the machines, nor were we in a good state to raise more capital. For few days, I walked the factory floor on what others saw as my routine walk, only that at those times, I was "speaking" to the machines, proclaiming divine intervention, wisdom, and necessary strategy.

In the meantime, the production and maintenance crew continued their schedules as normal. Shortly after, and assuredly, there was divine intervention. It was my way of getting wise counsel in WISDOM and STRATEGY. I learned firsthand what Solomon, the writer of Proverbs, meant when he said:

For by **strategy** *war is waged, and victory depends on many counselors* **(wisdom)**.

Proverbs 24:6-7 (NABRE)

If you want your business to be relevant, succeed, grow, and scale far into the future, I counsel you to follow these five steps. And if you want to get these results even faster, **I invite you to book a free 1-on-1 "*Dancing With The Stars Session*" with me** at IDEASDefinition@gmail.com

During this quick call, we'll look at your background, experience, and current situation, and we'll see what's possible for you in terms of how to grow and scale your business over next three months. We'll examine what you're doing now and find out what's working and what's not. We will identify the number one thing holding you back from having the enduring success you expect and map out a plan to get you where you want to go—faster. You'll leave the call feeling clear, confident, and excited about taking your business to the next level.

Like the human creation, every business fills a space in the divine order, in meeting the needs of the community they are in or operate in. Such a business is a GIFT to that world! And like a jigsaw, you and your business were prepared by God in such a way that you were dedicated to fit in at a particular spot. You were not meant to fit in someone else's spot, and no one else should fit in yours. It is true that... "after God formed you (and your enterprise) He discarded the mold." So, there are no duplicates of you or your enterprise.

You only need to K-N-O-W/discover where you are in God's

blueprint and function in in that place according to his plan.

I help Christian entrepreneurs that need assurance of their part in the divine Masterplan realize **relevance**, attain **success**, as well as enable **growth** and **sustainability**—into the future.

To schedule your free *"Dancing With The Stars Session"* **with me, go to** IDEASDefinition@gmail.com

----

------- T W O -------

Why is a religious organization classified as a business?

According to https://www.gen4christ.com/ministry-or-business an organization means:

"an administrative and functional structure (such as a business or a political party)"

It also says that a ministry is an organization that comes alongside the church to provide a service to meet people's needs, advance the gospel, build the Kingdom, and glorify God.

And the definition of a business?

The Miriam Webster Dictionary defines business as:

"usually commercial or mercantile activity engaged in as a means of livelihood."

Commercial and mercantile activities involve the production of goods for, or the provision of services to a customer. "Goods are produced, and services rendered, to meet people's needs." There is an exchange of money or items of value in return for these products or services. The exchange provides a means of livelihood (i.e., "A means of support or subsistence").

A business is an organization that provides a product or service that meets the needs of others in exchange for money or other valuable goods and services that foster the subsistence of both the provider and the customer.

Simply put… even though both ministry and business provide services to meet people's needs, they differ in their purposes: one to advance the gospel and glorify God and the other not necessarily so, in the secular context. Primarily, a business exists to serve people and meet their needs, but it may not be doing it to advance the gospel, build the Kingdom. and glorify God. A business' efforts are geared towards achieving its mission. Making money just happens to be an outcome of the efforts.

To the believer, a ministry and a business ought to be run in the very same way: efficiently, profitably, ethically, meeting the needs of the people they serve and by all means glorifying God.

Without doubt, Churches provide "services" in their community. "Though called charitable services, society benefits immensely- whether it be relief efforts like the feeding of the hungry, the clothing of the less privileged or discipling parishioners in the community to live ethically and make helpful contributions to society. These are priceless services rendered by the Church.

It is an undeniable fact that Churches are businesses and contribute a pretty good deal to society by themselves and through their parishioners.

Churches around the world and indeed in the United States may not be for-profit businesses, they are nonetheless recognized as performing "corporate activities" because of the benefits that the public derives. In appreciation of the services contributed by the Churches, tax exempt status was accorded them and made official in 1894 in the United States. It further received legal backing by the US Supreme Court's decision of January 14th, 1924 (*Trinidad vs. Sagrada Orden*).

------- T H R E E -------

Who is an Entrepreneur?

We frequently use the term "entrepreneur" rather loosely in today's business world. Given how frequently people give themselves or others this title, it is the kind of title that is fraught with emptiness. The truth is that those who truly embody the entrepreneurial spirit are those who are invested in and committed to causes that go far beyond themselves.

They successfully combine their passions and business expertise to create organizations that not only survive but positively affect the environment and the community in which they operate.

So much work has to be done behind the scenes, including planning, strategy, and committed execution that make up a large part of becoming an entrepreneur.

Finding inspiration, spiritual confirmation, researching and experimenting, talking with and hearing from people on what they believe is your expertise and considering their advice—all of these are necessary before coming up with that good and potentially "profitable" enterprise or ministry.

The business and ministry world is vast, and there are several leaders from whom you could and should learn. Every person in business or ministry faces comparable challenges such as hard work, devotion, time management, clear vision, and so on. Great leaders' paths to success are usually not easy, neither are all of them endowed with a silver spoon or vast corporate fortune. Find one whose lifestyle resonates with you and learn from that person. Also learn biblical principles about perseverance, commitment, and dedication to purpose.

The ultimate dream for so many of us is to be our own boss and by so doing, confidently fulfill God's call upon our lives.

A short while ago, I asked a few of my friends their opinion of who they thought an entrepreneur is. What I was exploring in the brief study was mainly how entrepreneurial skills are discovered and applied in the market place, including the Christian ministry.

One definition resonated and still resonates so very much with me that I have decided to share it here. According to one of them, "…an entrepreneur is that man (or woman) who remains charming and persistent while promoting his (or her) wares/services, even in the face of seeming negative influences, until he (or she) succeeds in getting sustainable patronage…"

There are quite a number of qualities packed into my friend's definition that would take few lines to unpack, which in my opinion, are compelling and necessary in identifying who that ideal entrepreneur is…

The words: "*remains*," i.e. undeterred; "*charming*," i.e. pleasant, not distracted by opposition; "*persistent*," i.e. enduring the heat of the game; "*promoting his wares/services*," i.e. not allowing anyone tell him or accepting anything different about his success; "*in the face of seeming negative influences*," i.e. unwavering, steadfast; "*until he succeeds*," i.e. continuing to push forward; "*getting sustainable patronage*," i.e. for now and later – into the future; all paint the picture of someone who is ready to *make a determined difference to a world that is eagerly waiting.*

That certainly looks to me the ideal entrepreneur:

i.   He/she finds the time to do what s/he sets out to achieve – no matter what.

ii. If s/he believes in a vision, s/he finds the passion and motivation to persevere until it is realized.

iii. He/she sees possibilities in every opportunity s/he ventures in and would not be deterred.

iv. He/she sets himself/herself to be determined and believable.

The doggedness of the ideal entrepreneur should not blind him/her to the need for constant reassessment of what has been done and what lies ahead, to ensure that s/he avoids past mistakes and is on the desired "proven" course.

And for the Christian in particular, it calls for continued prayers at every stage.

Archbishop Benson Idahosa of blessed memory would probably not end any counsel without the slogan: "*prayerful preparation prevents poor performance…*"

To be successful, the Christian entrepreneur must develop the habit of sustained PRAYING (Philippians 4:6).

------- F O U R -------

Tips For Starting Your Own Business or Ministry and Avoiding Failures

The recent COVID pandemic and the need to work from home has spurred many into thinking of starting their own businesses. Several people are coming up with amazing ideas of how to get into what they call their "own business," while several others have continued to explore how they could scale their existing businesses despite the pandemic realities.

Whichever is your situation, there are always some benefits to either starting your own business or modifying/pivoting and/or scaling an existing one.

This section will help guide your thoughts on the approaches to successful implementation.

I am not unmindful of the fact that there are those that are cut out to be business-owners and there are those that have the abilities to work in the businesses. One common denominator, however, is "entrepreneurial skills" which I consider as non-negotiable exists at both ends.

Also, a situation where all are "chiefs and no Indians" cannot be sustained long-term.

I am nonetheless guided by the belief that every Christian business, including enterprise or ministry is "inspired" of God, or ought to be, to meet the needs of particular people, in a particular geography and at a particular season. How the business or ministry functions to impact the world on a larger scale can be by divine orchestration and certainly through lots of marketing.

When beginning your own business, you likely will receive suggestions from family members, friends, and other well-wishers. Some of these will be well-intentioned and possibly workable. However, nothing will equal your very own due diligence since you have chosen the lofty path of owning or scaling your own business.

With that, let's consider some excellent recommendations that will work in your business, offered by a business leader.

1. Conduct Market Research

Now that you know what business you want to do, spend some quality time researching what is involved: what need(s) you are trying to fulfill; who are the target patrons; what are the likely associated costs; who else is in the market offering the same or a similar product or service; what they are selling at; what segment you intend to target; what integrated opportunities are available for sustainability; what would be your involvement; who you may need, to make your vision a reality and at what cost; and a whole myriad of other considerations including location and proximity to market. Market research will give you a bird's eye view of what to expect and help you know whether your concept has a competitive advantage in the chosen niche and whether there is money to be made.

And just by the way… there should be no reason to fall into the common delusion of thinking that there has never been anyone that has come up with your very idea or something like it. If you look hard enough, there have been, around the world, or there possibly still are, in distant or nearby places, someone or an organization doing the very same or something close enough to your proposition. Conduct market research!

2. Have a Vision

Every business starts with imagination. When imagination gets strong enough, it translates into a vision. By then it has gone past a mere mental picture into what you really want to see happen: what kind of organization you are setting up; how long will it be in existence; who will it benefit; what will be the working culture; etc.

Plan for how you want your company to grow. Write out your short- and long-term goals, as well as the time frame in which you expect them to be met. This will make life easier in the long term and ensures your business' sustainability.

3. Shop Your Competitors

Learning about your competitors and their consumers' demand pattern—who they serve, where they procure their product/ service input (raw materials), and at what costs—will assist you in discovering opportunities in market gaps. Your analysis of the competition may reveal other interesting, untapped opportunities that are available to you, which may help in positioning your new business for sustainable competitiveness both in the short and medium term.

The main focus here is to understand the business and to seek to be better than the competition, if and where you can.

4. Finance Your Company

This is the most important stage before beginning any business. You must determine your financial situation and how you will handle it. There are business financiers that will be happy to assist, including private and public funding. If you don't have enough money to start your business, you'll need to raise or borrow money.

Whether starting a new business with your money or someone else's, I am an advocate for prudency and integrity. A common pitfall in money matters is the lack of accountability.

5. What's In A Business Name?

From my several years of working with start-ups, one major challenge that new business owners face is that of giving the "right" name to their businesses.

A name is an identity, and a good and right name is a good identity!

So, what's in a name? Fortunately, everything. The Bible is replete with stories of names that were given by God before birth, some were changed at adulthood and yet others had to be changed - circumstantially:

For example, God named Ishmael, before birth (Genesis 16:11); Isaac, before birth (Genesis 17:19); Solomon, before birth (I Chronicles 22:9); Josiah, before birth (I Kings 13:2); Cyrus, before birth (Isaiah 44:28); John the Baptist, before birth (Luke 1:13); and Jesus Christ, before birth (Matthew 1:21).

God changed Abram's name, at adulthood, to Abraham – i.e.

father of many nations; Sarai's at adulthood, to Sarah – i.e. noble woman or princess; Jacob's at adulthood, to Israel – i.e. one who prevails with God; and Simon's at adulthood, to Peter – i.e. rock.

These people's lives changed their life stories for time and eternity. They had significant encounters with and interventions by God.

The Christian reading this will remember the story of a man called Jabez in I Chronicles 4, verses 9 and 10.

The names of businesses and or ministries, just like those of the individuals that I listed, mean so very much and must not be treated lightly.

Think through. Think hard. Pray through. Pray hard. Find a name that best describes what your business is all about; what you want it to represent: not one that is tongue-twisting or long or depicting some failures (past, present or future); not a name suggesting any form of limitation or discrimination; but a name that characterizes your image of the business: short enough, yet easy to say, easy to write and easy to remember.

It is equally important to give serious thought to what "structure" you would want your business to be: e.g. for-profit, as Limited Liability Company as Corporation (C or S); or as non-profit.

I suggest that you consult a tax expert on which business structure best suits your vision and on how to obtain required permits and licenses.

6. Have The Right Team:

Many well-meaning new business starters have been cut short by the team that they work with.

A business with the wrong set of leadership teams – in-house, and on the Board does not have a promised future.

Care has to be taken to choose the right and committed professionals on the job and the disciplined advisors and guides on the Board, who have a shared future goal: i.e. the success of the business is "our" success.

Business owners owe it a duty to ensure that the picture that they paint of the business and its future outlines not only sustainable goals but convincingly realistic and achievable targets, that motivate them and the team. It is these that translate into lasting and effective communications and affectionate relationships.

7. Euphoria, Passion, Inspiration:

Most new business starters will admit that they have gone through at least two of these three-some: euphoria, passion, and inspiration.

Most Christian new business owners will readily acknowledge that they have gone through all three. The thought of birthing a new business brings ecstasy. That excitement could last a while until the first couple of challenges.

Then comes along passion, produced by a strong faith in the new-found vision. Coupled with the determination to "endure" beyond challenges, passion sustains the vision and the visioner.

Inspiration, on the other hand, transcends the fleeting sensation, to give meaning to both euphoria and passion, longer term – in the new opportunity. It confronts challenges, sufferings and anxieties that might afflict the business - with endurance.

It is inspiration that encourages and emboldens the resolve to keep going, after doing due diligence, convinced that "tough times don't last; tough people do."

A business owner must learn to work and stay constantly inspired or s/he will be tempted to throw in the towel sooner than later.

Common Challenges Every Business/Ministry Faces

Small businesses, including ministries, face several challenges in their initial years of operation. Some of these obstacles are more difficult to overcome than others. According to one study, 20% of small businesses fail by the end of the first year. 50% fail by the end of their fifth year, and as many as 96% fail by the end of their tenth-year.

These rates are alarming. It's understandable why people are anxious about the first few years of a business. However, many typical business issues and difficulties are resolvable. If you want your business to grow and prosper, you must be aware of and adept at avoiding the common pitfalls of growth. You must ensure that your actions today don't end up causing more issues tomorrow. Not resolving clientele's issues or not resolving them soon enough could threaten the organization's long-term existence.

Also, making the most of the opportunities that are available to you today, in effectively meeting needs, will facilitate long-term, sustainable growth.

To save you from trouble, here are a few challenges that may arise in any business and what you need to do to face them before they knock at the door.

3 Most Common Business/Ministry Challenges

1. Finding and keeping patrons: clients, congregants.

Finding patrons is an issue that isn't exclusive to small businesses; even the biggest, most prosperous businesses employ individuals who work tirelessly every day and night to find new clients. The problem is far more severe for small businesses and start-ups. And perhaps common to both big and small enterprises is the task of keeping them.

There are a lot of channels for acquisition of clients and leads to concentrate on, but how you decide which ones to prioritize and how to maintain/sustain them is vital to the businesses' survival. First and foremost is to identify who your target clients are. Then, your business performance will be significantly enhanced by developing an identity, culture, and values.

2. Managing Finances

One of several qualities that separates the successful from the pack is their ability to carefully manage their finances. You need effective cash flow management, to ensure that what goes out is lower than what comes in. Cash shortages can be the most significant factor limiting growth. Planning for your business and evaluating new opportunities should include making the most of your current and available cash.

Co-mingling personal and business finances usually leads to unexpected disaster and is to be avoided.

3. **Accepting change**

A growing company may face severe risks from complacency and indifference. It isn't smart thinking to assume your success will continue just because you have managed to stay in business till now. Your business plan should be reviewed and updated regularly to keep you informed of the dynamic market conditions. It is your responsibility to adapt to current market trends.

------- F I V E -------

Create a Business Plan

Every time that I hear the slogan "They who fail to plan, plan to fail," I am reminded of the imaginary story of the commercial pilot who, after boarding the plane began to ask his passengers where each of them was going. The first few told him where they were going, but after they saw the surprised look on the pilot's face, and in apparent fear that he was clueless, they quickly turned around and asked to disembark the plane. Several others who were told what just transpired followed suit and disembarked. The airline failed. The pilot failed. And by trickle-down effect, the investors failed.

Every commercial plane is supposed to have a destination chart and schedule, against which the airline advertises and sells flight tickets. Of course, details of that chart include the flight plan. They have a duty to ensure that the pilot knows the plan and will execute it. Even though this story is farfetched, if the airline fails to plan, it is a sure indication that they plan to fail.

Plus… there usually are different plans you need to put in place as you go along: an establishment plan, a production plan, a management plan, sales and marketing plans, growth/expansion/contraction plans, etc. Sometimes these plans could last a while, other times, they become dynamic, needing to change with circumstances.

Realizing how important plans are to any enterprise, be it a ministry or other ventures, is there any wonder that banks refuse, as their cardinal condition, to look at funding requests that are without plans?

A **business plan or feasibility study,** as some might refer to it, lays out the steps you must take for a successful launch and ongoing growth.

Think of the business plan as your GPS to guide your journey, so you have the necessary direction to help you get to desired destination.

A business plan ensures that you present your company in the best possible light to other professionals who are evaluating it.

Your business plan must present clear, concise, and easy-to-understand content for your review, from time to time, and be able to turn your "would-be" to "can-do."

Part of that plan includes a financial plan, that should show sources of capital, from personal savings, friends and family, angel investors, venture capitalists as well as the Small Business Association (SBA), or any other, as applicable.

------- S I X -------

Running Your Business With The Future In Focus.

We all need to work on making our enterprise profitable among the competition. Many startup businesses and ministries lose their success because of the failure they face at the start and after their breakthrough. No matter how good a sales and marketing team you hire might be, staying relevant in the corporate world has never been a piece of cake.

To make your enterprise relevant, flourish, and sustainable, here are a few things you can do:

1. Keep your enterprise updated with new trends.

We all know that staying contemporary is the key to the success of many Fortune-500 companies. If we evolve with time, we may become the next big thing. Try to hire innovative people and individuals with a broader picture of the future.

2. Study your competitors.

To compete in the corporate world, you must analyze in as much detail, the moves of your competitors, learning how they deal with their clients, sales, and what makes them relevant in the marketplace. Shop the competition.

3. Stay in the present.

Rather than thinking about the future clients and mistakes you have made with past clients, try to stay in the present and work on the things that require your current attention. Find flaws that have led your startup business or ministry to have low patronage. Instead of making a big target, make several small goals and work on them successfully.

4. Know your product or service: price it right.

Know everything that needs to be known about your product or service. Price it right: neither underprice nor overprice. Realize that you are in the marketplace with competition waiting to take your clientele.

How to succeed, grow, and sustain your business-ministry.

At some point in the entrepreneur's life, they must have considered starting a business. Sadly, over a 10-year period, statistics show that only 4% of such start-ups stand the chance of survival. Several factors are responsible for such a high failure rate.

It is important that you come to grips with the dynamics of owning a business and how to realize success and avoid failures.

Four Qualities Needed To Succeed As an Entrepreneur

Being a successful entrepreneur requires more than just having a good idea, even though it continues to be one essential component. There are few other prerequisites.

Not everyone will naturally have an entrepreneurial mindset; the principles and processes can be learned. Here are the four key qualities that a person must possess in order to succeed as an entrepreneur.

1. **Be convinced and enthusiastic about what you want to accomplish.**

Even if they know what they want to do, new entrepreneurs frequently struggle to find the right fit, many times because they have not quite listened to God nor done due diligence. It's critical to assess your level of passion for your intended endeavor if you're thinking about starting an enterprise. A lack of enthusiasm and conviction can spell disaster right from the onset.

2. **Implement your ideas.**

In any enterprise, the execution of ideas is the most crucial element. Even if you have the best idea and the money to implement it, your enterprise won't succeed if it remains "good idea" in the cooler or on the drawing table. Neither does it stand any chance of survival if it cannot be implemented with some level of excellence.

3. **Learn, Learn, & Learn!**

You must simply love learning if you want to be an entrepreneur. Running an enterprise can be challenging, especially when you first start out. Every day, you'll run into unforeseen issues, and you won't always be able to figure out the best way to handle them. When things don't go according to plan, your ability to learn new things quickly will help you make wiser decisions. You won't always know the solutions, and there will be times when you need to step back and reconsider a strategy that isn't working, but overall, learning is always invaluable—even from failures.

4. Create a Network

Nobody has ever achieved success on their own. Each and every entrepreneur who has achieved success has benefited from a network of mentors, associates, workers, and investors that are willing and ready to help you. Getting expert assistance will always have a big impact on your enterprise.

How To Make Your business startup and Ministry successful

Making your business startup or ministry successful takes more than guts to achieve, but it becomes more challenging when you have no prior experience or skill in managing the dynamics of what you are setting out to do. Many people end up in debts from loans taken to start their enterprise, which rather unfortunately, failed to yield desired results.

Here are a few things to keep in mind, when starting your business or ministry:

1. **Have clarity** on what it is you want to do or accomplish.

2. **Be ready to commit** time, energy, focus and resources to discovering what is needed and be innovative in providing it.

3. **Trust the established process. Use your business plan. Manage your enterprise, not the other way around. For better outcomes, take the** sure and steady path rather than the enticing shortcuts towards success.

4. **Have faith and stay consistent.** You can achieve more

when you stay consistent and have faith in whatever you do. Do not let the fire of your passion go out.

5. Never be afraid to make mistakes. **Learn from mistakes**—from yours and those in similar enterprise. Make efforts to avoid being a statistic.

6. **Find hand-holders**, guides, mentors, coaches, that will motivate you through the uncharted journey until your mission is realized.

Put simply, to have an enduring success:

» stay on the path to working and making your goal succeed. Give it your time, energy, focus and resources.

» have faith. Find your spark and keep it alive.

Ways to Scale Your Business or Ministry in A Competitive Market

To be successful in today's ultra-competitive market, businesses and ministries must be adaptable and imaginative. This can be accomplished through changing the model, planning, getting creative, and thinking critically. Because the economy is so uncertain, businesses must adapt in every manner suited to their situation, ethically and professionally. Companies that are prepared and equipped to deal with unexpected market developments tend to do better than those that do not.

It takes time to cut through the competition and make your brand recognized in the market. You will need to create a blueprint of what and how you want things to operate. Of course, good planning entails properly managing products, processes, supply chains, and marketing. These factors together will assist you in rapidly and successfully growing your organization by staying ahead of competition.

1. Understand Your Products, Service or Ministry

The things or services you provide are the bedrock of your business, and it is through them that you can urge people to return for more. You will need to learn all there is to know about your products or services, so you can assist consumers with any questions they may have. Knowing your product also means that you can adequately describe it, position it in the right market category, and market it to the right clients.

2. Build Thoughtful Approaches

Entrepreneurs spend quite a lot of effort developing procedures and approaches that work for them. There are procedures that are short-term and others that are medium- and long-term. Entrepreneurs must think longer term for sustainability but must think short and medium term in response to market changes. They must ensure that customers are easily able to engage with them and the products or services they offer. That way, they understand first-hand the dictates of the market they serve and customize their approaches to them.

3. Profit from the Cutting Edge

Discerning business and ministry owners know that there are competitors out in the market that are doing well: perhaps better than they are. To differentiate your brand from the competition and to further scale the enterprise, an entrepreneur must be familiar and periodically conduct a **SWOT** (Strengths/ Weaknesses/Opportunities/Threats) and **PESTLE** (*Political, Economic, Social, Technological, Legal and Environmental*) analysis. They must take advantage of contemporary technology including communications/social media and industry terminology. This will enable the owner to realize otherwise neglected opportunities and to adjust, when and where necessary. Identifying, developing, and selling your enterprise's capabilities are what today's cutting edge technologies are marketed to provide—for success, scaling, and sustainability.

4. Break-Even; Flat Run

Every enterprise owner goes through stages when he or she produces at a break-even point. The business makes neither a loss nor profit. The revenue just matches production costs. This can and should only be temporary, because after gaining the trust of clients and with increased sales, the business owner has the opportunity of scaling upwards, for long-term sustainability. The concept of managing your enterprise with a "flat" organizational structure is quite similar. This new trend is catching on among start-ups. For newbies, a "vertical" management hierarchy with many layers of authority appears no longer fashionable. Instead, a "horizontal" management practice that encourages every worker to make direct and hands-on contribution to the success of the enterprise is gaining increased acceptance.

5. Talk and Walk like a Millennial

The current generation values freedom and a high and better standard of living; therefore, you must adapt to take advantage of their lifestyle. Your product must be appealing to trending generations, to gain their patronage. A millennial-friendly business will court and obtain millennial patronage.

Cutting through the clutter and the noise of competitors could be overwhelming, but responding to the dictates of the trending market has never been wrong.

Status Quo In A Business or Ministry and How To Break Free from It

Status quo is an enterprise's slow killer, yet many entrepreneurs are unaware of it or the developments that lead to it. A business is considered in status quo when the current or existing condition of affairs remains just the "same old, same old" with nothing changing.

To the simple-minded, the status quo situation is always the easy way out. It is the comfort zone. How nice it would be if we could all simply just keep things the same and not change. But the status quo has always been a trap that does no sustaining good. The "comfort zone" could easily become the "coffin zone" by the way of status quo.

The corporate world is always evolving. Customers change purchasing patterns, markets change positions, seasons influence patronage, rivals change products/prices, and economic insecurity alters everything. As a result, maintaining the status quo is no longer sufficient, and companies must learn to adapt and evolve. It does not take long before the spark that motivated the entrepreneur wears off and they begin to feel slavish when at work and relieved when off-work. They are in a rut and feel blind to the way out of it, having lost the mojo that once helped start the business in the first place. It is a state of tail-chasing, with little or nothing to show for all the effort.

This brings up the notion of anti-status quo or refusing to accept the status quo. In it, you make wise judgments and take calculated steps to break away from the current state.

The following are three reasons why businesses become trapped in a rut:

1. Lack of clarity

Over time, organizations lose their sense of direction and divert into virtually every "perceived" profitable avenue. This is why you must have defined goals that are also conveyed to stakeholders: investors, workers, as well as customers so that they are aware of the brand and culture. Define your business's value proposition and be sure your staff understand the culture and the core of the business so they can embrace them and create interesting approaches around them.

2. Risk aversion

The business owner who chooses security of investment over the potential for higher-than-average return will likely not make much progress, not to talk of scaling. While irresponsible risk could ruin your business or ministry and keep you in status quo, being overly conservative will very possibly make you feel old and stuck as well. Most conservative business owners have the inclination to agree to a situation with a more predictable, but possibly lower payoff, rather than a situation with a highly unpredictable, but possibly higher payoff. When you make necessary adjustments in risky situations that enables your business to stay alive, you will save yourself from needless stress and ultimate failure.

3. Lack of Accountability

A status quo position also occurs when people are not held accountable for their conduct. Employees make their own judgments without seeking the business owner's or their trusted leaders' concurrence. It is the obligation of the entrepreneur or their trusted representatives to explain to staff what is expected of them and to put in place a fair reward system for meeting expectations, both in terms of productivity as well as accountability.

------- SEVEN -------

Look for a Helper, a Guide, a Mentor, a Business Advisor.

In my book: "You Can Make A Determined Difference …In An Environment Of Competitiveness," I cover the need for a helper along life's journey a bit more in- depth.

Suffice to say that there is far more need, in business and or ministry, for a helper than outside of it.

That is the reason why associations, unions, alliances are formed: for one inestimable reason: getting help.

No matter how good you consider yourself to be at what you do, you cannot afford to discount the importance of getting help – if you must go far.

My mother, of sweet memory, often calls her children and in warning, prayed "May people never point to your failure for what to avoid."

It was obvious to my mom that if we don't compare our actions with others and learn from them, we are susceptible to becoming the bad lesson others should avoid. That philosophy, sad to say, is more pertinent in today's business rat-race than any other time. And who really wants his/her business to fail – like that other one… we can't even now remember the name? I, for one, would rather wish that others point to my successes, for emulation.

Avoid being a statistic: seek a business helper, a guide, a mentor, or an advisor. If you have the right mutual chemistry with the helper, you can be rest assured that your association will also be of tremendous mutual benefit. And if your chemistry with one does not seem cordial or helpful, you should never hesitate to cut ties and seek another.

Just know that mentoring should never feel like a trap, or the essential trust in the relationship is lost.

No matter how appealing it may sound, starting an enterprise shouldn't be an independent, lonely, endeavor. You can improve your chances of success by finding people who have already taken the journey that you are now embarking on and asking their counsel and direction. Connect with other professionals in the industry, attend workshops and events tailored to your sector, and get in touch with successful thought leaders to understand their methodology.

New starters find out that there are a thousand things to work on at once. Newbies cannot escape this reality, but with some preparation, it is possible to focus on necessities, control expectations and take deliberate steps to succeed, maintain, and scale the business and brand. Juggling several balls in the air at the same time demands skill and getting the understanding of "how to" that could be learned from those who are more adept at doing it (i.e. mentors) could be a valuable asset, to anyone starting a new business.

You can rest assured that there is abundant help out there, if you dare to ask, including organizations like IDEAS DEFINITION GLOBAL, that are on a mission to assist business owners struggling with failure and sustainability. We work with various sectors, including manufacturing, services, for-profit and nonprofits, and are able to help organizations move forward by implementing the necessary growth strategies.

We have firsthand knowledge of the universal desire among entrepreneurs to expand and improve their companies. We understand that only a small number consciously take the necessary steps to turn their desires into reality.

IDEAS DEFINITION GLOBAL can be reached at IDEASDefinition@gmail.com

I also strongly recommend reading Principle 6 of my book YOU CAN MAKE A DETERMINED DIFFERENCE … In An Environment Of Competitiveness for a much more detailed discussion and guidance on seeking help.

www.ingramcontent.com/pod-product-compliance
Lightning Source LLC
Chambersburg PA
CBHW040910210326
41597CB00029B/5031